D0646959

SHARING THE PLEASURES OF READING

Sharing the Pleasures

# of Reading

WELLERAN POLTARNEES

YEAR 2000

DARLING & COMPANY

DARLING AND COMPANY POST OFFICE BOX 4399 **SEATTLE** WASHINGTON 98104

COPYRIGHT © 2000 BLUE LANTERN STUDIO

FIRST PRINTING. ALL RIGHTS RESERVED

ISBN 1-883211-24-7

PRINTED IN SINGAPORE

H umankind began the long journey of language development with spoken words. People communicated for many millennia before there was any thought of writing or reading. As it was for humanity so it is for each of us—we begin by finding meaning in spoken sounds and by learning to make our vocalizations intelligible. By these skills we conquer our isolation and learn what others think and want. When speaking and listening has been learned we turn to reading and writing.

For the ancient Greeks reading was, according to Moses Hadas, "Something to be listened to rather than something to be scanned silently in private." Alberto Manguel observes in *A History of Reading* (1996): "Until well into the Middle Ages, writers assumed that their readers would hear rather than simply see the text, much as they themselves spoke their words out loud as they composed them. Since comparatively few people could read, public readings were common, and medieval texts repeatedly call upon the audience to 'lend ears' to a tale."

The differences between reading aloud and silently are many and profound. The one is a public act in which the reader is revealed with their strengths and weaknesses. Silent reading is profoundly introspective, so much so that many readers do not hear or see what is going on in the room where they are. Many who read aloud move rhythmically, their faces reflecting the emotions evoked by the words—these things helping to involve and convince the listeners. Stephen King, in the novel *IT* (1986) conjures this power: "The Children's Library was bright and sunny, a little noisier in spite of the LET'S BE QUIET, SHALL WE? signs that were posted around. Most of the noise usually came from Pooh's Corner, where the little kids went to look at picture-books. When Ben came in today, story hour had just begun there. Miss Davies, the pretty young librarian, was reading "The Three Billy Goats Gruff."

'Who is that trip-trapping upon my bridge?'

Miss Davies spoke in the low, growling tones of the troll in the story. Some of the little ones covered their mouths and giggled, but most only watched her solemnly, accepting the voice of the troll as they accepted the voices in their dreams, and their grave eyes reflected the eternal fascination of the fairy tale."

The reason that theater excites in a way that a recorded performance does not is that living beings, in our place and time, manifest themselves in order to convince and entertain. If the identical performance was filmed and played back to the same audience it

would have nothing like the same impact. So it is with reading aloud. The presence of a reader, the giving of themselves, adds enormously to the listeners' enjoyment.

Reading aloud is not simply a matter of active reader and passive listener. There is a continuing interaction between them in which both contribute to the experience. Sean Wilentz remarks: "You the reader, aided by your sidekick, are free to do just about anything, changing tempos, cutting lines, adding new ones, departing from the text entirely. As the child's breath thickens and there's a yawn or two, you might wind down to the softest of codas, or end abruptly, leaving the story line hanging at just the right spot, till next time. In short, free improv: reading to kids is to ordinary reading what jazz is to a string quartet."

The very willingness to read aloud, the choice of what is to be read, how the words are spoken, and kinds of feeling with which the reader creates—all of these are self revelations. The listener also makes a gift of vulnerability—they open themselves to the experience.

Reading aloud is an affirmation of the power of the book. We all have available a myriad of recreational choices, and our selection among them is meaningful.

This volume is one of a series of publications utilizing the Blue Lantern Library of children's books. This library, which includes about ten thousands books, emphasizes excellence or individuality in illustration, especially as found in children's books published before 1940. Picture from this library were reproduced for many years by The Green Tiger Press, in books and on a variety of stationary products. Since 1992 The Laughing Elephant, another publishing company, has similarly utilized this resource. Recently we

have come to the conclusion that the piecemeal sharing of this imagery, though useful and successful, presents an inadequate view of the vast wealth contained in old children's books, and that a more analytical approach would be a valuable supplement to our activities. The first manifestation of this impulse was the book *From Mother Goose to Dr. Seuss: Children's Book Covers 1860-1960*, which was published in 1999 by Chronicle Books. Though books from various publishers may continue to appear, the focus of our efforts will continue to be through The Laughing Elephant and its sister publishing venture Darling and Co.

We selected children's book covers as our first analytic effort because the covers are the first things one encounters. This, our second study, is about the next step of encounter, when we ask others to share with us the excitement of our discovery.

— Welleran Poltarnees and the staff of The Blue Lantern Library

reading together

When we see something amazing we call others to look at it with us. It can be bad or good, but humans wish to share moments of importance. We call our fellows to the window to see lightning fill the field; we pass a letter bearing bad news from hand to hand; when we receive a surprise package we open it together. Yet it is not just the unexpected we wish to share—everyday events like a puppy chasing a shadow, or a child fallen asleep on the floor are as likely to gather a crowd as a burst pipe in our kitchens.

I learned from the age of two or three that any room in our house, at any time of day, was there to read in, or to be read to. My mother read to me. She'd read to me in the big bedroom in the mornings, when we were in her rocker together, which ticked in rhythm as we rocked, as though we had a cricket accompanying the story. She'd read to me in the dining-room on winter afternoons in front of the coal fire, with our cuckoo clock ending the story with "Cuckoo," and at night when I'd got in my own bed. I must have given her no peace. Sometimes she read to me in the kitchen while she sat churning, and the churning sobbed along with *any* story.

—EUDORA WELTY

P icture books, and other beautiful objects, somehow demand to be shared. We speak aloud as we discover their virtues, and anyone in the room with us will come to our side to see what it is that excites such pleasure, and, with a picture book, once attracted they are likely to stay for the images need to be explored, and the pages as they are turned, enthrall us.

W hatever the picture-books a child gets, however, the intimate experience of sharing them with a parent is probably the most basically satisfying of the lot. From this safe vantage point, children can look at pictures that have the effect of slowing down normal experience, so that a child can take an isolated image on the page and then absorb or discuss it at leisure, gradually learning its most obvious characteristics.

—NICHOLAS TUCKER

R eading together encourages physical closeness. People lean together, sit close to one another, share laps, and even find themselves breathing in the same rhythm.

People like to go to museums with friends, even though they may not speak, but stand silent before the paintings. They enjoy going to movies with others, just to have someone enjoying the experience beside them in the darkness. Moments of intense apprehension are good to share.

I n looking at picture books together each looker tends to see different things. Adults see first the actions which advance the story. Children tend to see the odd things—the frog sitting in the shadow of the wall, the picture of two cows on the wall, the horse running outside of the open window, the torn pocket, the cracked window.

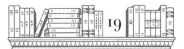

T he greatest fun in reading aloud lies in the adventure of the thing—the sense of taking a child on an exploration of a fascinating territory into which you alone have penetrated.

—LEONARD WIBBERLEY

Few children learn to love books by themselves. Someone has to lure them into the wonderful world of the written word; someone has to show them the way.

—ORVILLE PRESCOTT

The first poems I knew were nursery rhymes, and before I could read them for myself I had to come to love just the words of them, the words alone. What the words stood for, symbolized, or meant, was of the secondary importance; what mattered was the *sound* of them as I heard them for the first time on the lips of the remote and incomprehensible grown-ups who seemed, for some reason, to be living in my world. And these words were, to me, as the notes of bells, the sounds of musical instruments, the noises of wind, sea, and rain, the rattle of milkcarts, the clopping of hooves on cobbles, the fingering of branches on a window pane, might be to someone, deaf from birth, who has miraculously found his hearing. I did not care what the words said, overmuch, nor what happened to Jack & Jill & the Mother Goose rest of them; I cared for the shapes of sound that their names, and the words describing their actions, made in my ears; I cared for the colours the words cast on my eyes…I fell in love—that is the only expression I can think of—at once, and am still at the mercy of words.…

—DYLAN THOMAS

The favorite sounds of my remembered life are a single fiddle laying across a valley in the Alps, my wife humming to herself and my first daughter gurgling as she was bathed in a yellow dish pan, popping corn over a snapping campfire in the Sierras, old Smoky barking at my returning boat from a dock in the Thousand Islands, the all night song of a mockingbird on a sleepless night in Southern California, the ticking of a grandfather clock on the stairway of my grandmother's house, being waked by the buzz of bees after I had fallen asleep in a meadow, a hundred nights of rain on the roof and windows as I slept, and the sound of my mother's voice as she read *Kidnapped* to me when I was about eight years old.

—TIMOTHY CHURCH

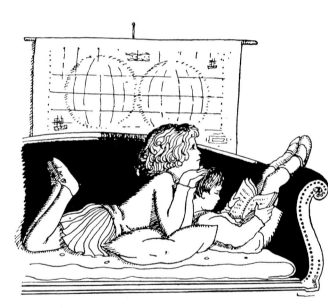

reading alou

Most of the tales of Hans Christian Andersen and the Brother's Grimm I heard by the time I was four years old. I heard them at dusk, which is the proper time of day to hear fairy tales. I heard them sitting at my mother's knee, which is the best place, the only place to sit when you leave the safe world you know for the unfamiliar and perilous world you don't know.

—SCOTT O'DELL

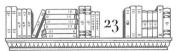

I f I close my eyes and concentrate, I can even now hear my mother's voice as she read to me each evening when I was a child—both picture books and poetry. I remember the cadences and inflections, the lilt and verve, of her special reading voice. Nuanced and expressive, it pronounced each word slowly and distinctly and lingered lovingly over syllables or phrases. Not at all like her normal "hurry-up" voice, this one had the capacity to transport me to faraway times and places, to send tremors through my spine, to conjure exotic pictures in my mind even as her fingers pointed to details of images on the pages of a book. Best of all, it embraced me with an auditory ambience of coziness and warmth. In those evening hours, we stretched and grew together. We could be anywhere, with anyone; it was anytime; I was sure I could do, or have, or feel anything; and then, when it was over and all the clouds of make-believe dissolved, the safety of her presence remained to hold me.

—ELLEN HANDLER SPITZ

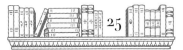

 A loved adult's voice conjuring up a colorful story-world…the memory evokes such warm and contented feelings as recollections of infant nursing might hold, if we could remember back that far. Indeed, the two experiences have common elements: the physical and emotional closeness of adult and child, the adult's attentiveness to the child, and the aim of satisfying a hunger. Clearly, both activities are nurturing ones.

—KIMMEL & SEGAL

You may have tangible wealth untold:
Caskets of jewels and coffers of gold.
Richer than I you can never be—
I had a Mother who read to me.

—STRICKLAND GILLILAN

H ow vividly most people remember the experience of being read to as children! They can tell you exactly whether it was mother or dad who read at bedtime. They know it was Aunt Lou who specialized in Kipling, and Mrs. Rossi in third grade who read *Charlotte's Web* the last thing every afternoon.

reading aloud

My mother usually somehow managed, at eleven, to sit down for half an hour in the red rocking chair by the window. She called this half hour her "respite," a word which early charmed me; and on days when no drafts were blowing across the floor (for even The Rising Sun was not always victorious over the worst of Maine weather) she would help us down from our Parnassus and allow us to sit upon our red stools while, our cookies and milk consumed, she herself would read aloud to us. Here was the very doorsill to complete enhancement, for she was seemingly as lost as we in whatever she was reading. The iron teakettle simmered on The Rising Sun; the red geraniums glowed with life; smells of our approaching dinner filled our noses from stewpans or baking dishes; while my mother's voice brought trooping into our kitchen all those with whom we rejoiced or suffered, admired or feared, loved or hated.

—MARY ELLEN CHASE

Anne Marie sat me down opposite her, on my little chair. She bent forward, lowered her eyelids, fell asleep. From that statue-like face came a plaster voice. I was bewildered: who was telling what and to whom? My mother had gone off: not a smile, not a sign of complicity, I was in exile. And besides, I didn't recognize her speech. Where had she got that assurance? A moment later, I realized: it was the book that was speaking. Frightening sentences emerged from it: they were real centipedes, they swarmed with syllables and letters, stretched their diphthongs, made the double consonants vibrate. Singing, nasal, broken by pauses and sighs, rich in unknown words, they were enchanted with themselves and their meanderings, without bothering about me. Sometimes they disappeared before I was able to understand them; at other times I understood in advance; and they continued to roll nobly to their end without sparing me a single comma.

—Jean-Paul Sartre

Whether one is confined to bed by a brief illness, or limited by more lingering ill health, they are likely to be hungry for stimulus from the outside world from which they are isolated. What lovelier escape than books which take us to places which even the healthiest cannot access, and open for us doors which otherwise would remain closed. Further, the sick one longs for companionship, too often listening to the sounds of a shared life in which they no longer seem to have a place. Sharing a book together not only provides human contact, but involves a mutual experience in which the reader and the listener experience together. Finally, books remind us at every moment of the power of the world and mind and spirit where even the weakest can soar, and the most limited can triumph.

reading to someone who is ill

I would settle down (at night, but also during the day, since frequent bouts of asthma kept me trapped in my bed for weeks) and, propped up high against the pillows, listen to my nurse read the Grimms' terrifying fairy-tales. Sometimes her voice put me to sleep; sometimes, on the contrary, it made me feverish with excitement, and I urged her on in order to find out, more quickly than the author had intended, what happened in the story. But most of the time I simply enjoyed the luxurious sensation of being carried away by the words, and felt, in a very physical sense, that I was actually travelling somewhere wonderfully remote, to a place that I hardly dared glimpse on the secret last page of the book.

—ALBERTO MANGUEL

C hildren are usually impressed with their powerlessness. They control few of the details of their destiny, and they know this. Because of this they treasure opportunities to show their skills, or manifest their power. Reading books is an especially satisfying skill, because we all know instinctively that this is one of the most advanced of human skills. Reading aloud to an adult is a profound accomplishment for a child because, through one's skills, a full-sized person is transported to other worlds, bathed in story and delighted by the power of the spoken word.

One of the great discoveries for the young reader is that the world becomes a much more comprehensible place with the help of books. By their use the vast welter of birds becomes a group of related bird families. Tools for which we have discovered no clear use are defined and made useful. In a fathomless sky of stars we can, with help, discern constellations. Trees, clouds, insects, rocks—all are better understood with a guidebook in hand. What we learn as a child is that the concrete world can be best discerned with the help of accumulated wisdom. This insight will broaden, as we grow, to include abstract matters such as what people are like, how societies operate, and even help to answer such questions as the purpose of existence.

How wonderful it is to share these discoveries with someone else, to have one read from the book while the other examines the shell it describes.

F rom kindergarten on I hated school. Almost everything about it disgusted me. I felt sick in the mornings when school awaited. I couldn't stomach food, but my mother forced me to eat. The streetcar ride was nearly unbearable, and when I arrived at school there was the overwhelming smell of salami sandwiches. I was abject at every subject. I couldn't learn the alphabet in proper order, or remember which combinations made which sounds, and numbers were even worse. I hated all the other children at recess, and did badly when made to play games. There was one bright moment each day: Miss Whitelow, our kindergarten teacher, had us put our heads down on our folded arms on our desks, and then she read to us from a book called *The Big Book of Stories and Fables*. With my eyes closed and her sweet voice reading, I skipped along with a group of animals setting out together to make their fortunes in the world. I saw the golden bird in the tree with golden apples and saw the arrows bounce harmlessly off of him. I went on the journey with the little boy no bigger than a thumb, and was frightened for the little rabbit who went hunting and caught the blazing sun in his trap. There in the classroom I escaped from my fears and dislikes into a world of wonder and adventure. I say, "Thank You, Miss Whitelow, for reading to us, for helping me to love books with their power to lift us out of ourselves into realms of delight."

R eading separately, yet together, is one of the greatest joys of friendship and family. There is no need for discussion. Each person does what they want to do, and the silent activities somehow weave into harmony. Sometimes one writes a letter while the other plays solitaire. Another time one writes in their diary and the other sews. Frequently one reads and the other writes or sorts or just thinks about the music they both enjoy. Best of all is when both read their own book. There together they venture forth into the many realms of the imagination, each taking a very different route, but each returning to that room with the ticking clock, turning to each other with a slight smile, and then launching forth onto a fresh journey.

We only had a few books in our house, and so we took turns reading them. My brother read *Huckleberry Finn* while I read *The Wind in the Willows*. Then we exchanged books. It was quiet, and whenever John chuckled, or gasped at something exciting I would look up and imagine what he was reading about. When I was reading about Huck's visit from his drunken father he was reading about Mole's first meeting Ratty. When Huck first goes on the river in his book Ratty is teaching Mole the true love of boats and water. From there on the two got mixed together in my mind. The vast Mississippi ran through the wood where the animals lived. The evil ferrets in my world mixed up with the duke and king in his. His triumphs became mine, and I think we both enjoyed our books with a quite unique relish.

—ARCHIBALD RAWLINGS

reading separately yet togethe

All three of us read everything that came our way, with uncritical zest. Often my father and I read the same book at the same time, his six feet three extended in an easy chair, my growing length draped against his chest. So I remember reading *The White Company, Harry Lorrequer, Allan Quartermain* by Rider Haggard. In this last book there was a young warrior named, I think, Umslopogaas, whom we very much admired. From this time, for many years, my father called me by this name. In fact, he had a variety of names for me, beginning from the time the news of my conception was first broken to him. The three of us, and, later, Caroline, had secret names for each other that the outside world never knew.

I think it was in these days, when first we began to read together, that the bond between my father and me strengthened into a deep understanding and we became the most loved of friends. As he waited for my slower grasp of the page to catch up to his, as his large shapely hand was raised to turn the page, a palpable emotion stirred within us.

—MAZO DE LA ROCHE

bedtime reading

My father died thirty-seven years ago when I was sixteen. My dearest and clearest memories of him are when he read to me from *The Book House* every evening. I remember each detail—the chair, the lamp, how I felt next to him, the way his eyes peered through his bifocals, the bit of saliva at the corner of his mouth, and, most of all, his voice. Fifty years later I still can hear exactly how he sounded . . . For those few minutes he was all mine, that voice was all for me.

—MARY VAN DYKE

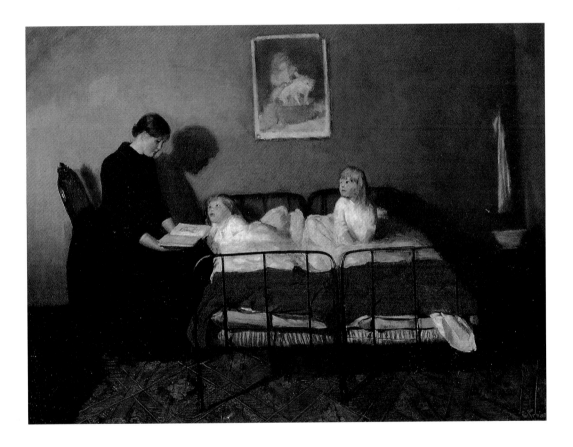

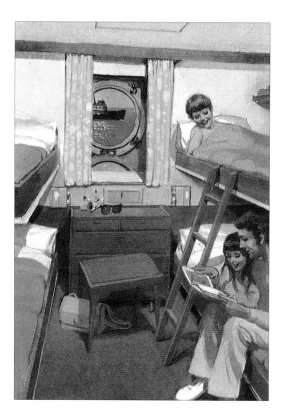

I n a dark room when a child is ready for bed, with the lamplight full on the pages of a book and his mind concentrated on a single voice, that of mother or father reading aloud from the great stories of the past, the child, on the edge of sleep, becomes again the unconscious recipient of the great imaginative currents of history. No new myths are created, but at least the great myths are kept alive. And the sensibility of the child is trained to cope with life's problems; he finds defenses against tragedy and words with which to express joy; his ear is developed to appreciate the subtleties of language and the mystery and power of words.

—WILLIAM JAY SMITH

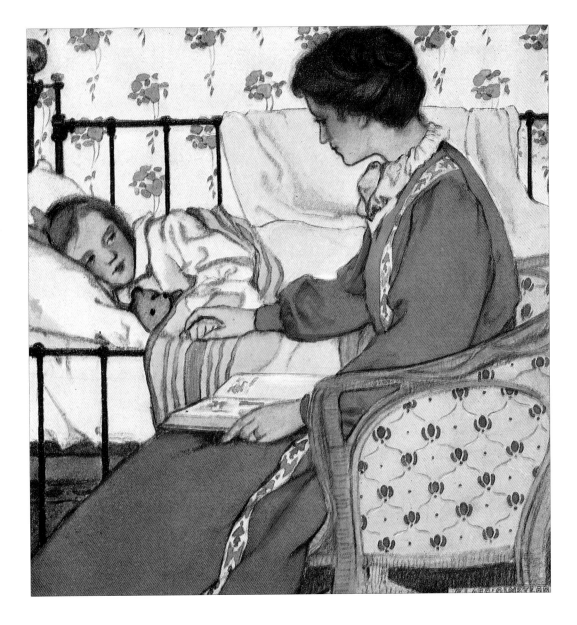

PICTURE CREDITS

Cover	Steve Johnson and Lou Fancher.
Endpapers	Nellie Farnam and Clarence Biers.
	From *David's Friends at School*, 1936.
Half-title left	Millicent Sowerby. From *Childhood*, 1907.
Half-title right	Jessie Willcox Smith. Magazine cover, 1921.
Frontispiece	Jessie Willcox Smith.
	From *Boys and Girls of Bookland*, 1923.
Title page	Emilie Benson Knipe. From *Remember Rhymes*, 1914.
Copyright	Helen Jacobs. From *Jolly Alphabets and Puzzles*, n.d.
5	James J. Shannon. Painting, n.d.
6	Unknown, n.d.
7	C.C. Chambers, "The Loved Ones at Home," 1932.
8	B. Cory Kilvert. From *The Kite Book*, 1909.
9	Cicely Mary Barker. From *At The Window*, c.1920.
10	Elizabeth Shippen Green. "The Five Little Pigs," n.d.
11	E. Phillips Fox. "The Lesson," c.1912.
12	Unknown. From *In Pictureland*, c.1906.
13	Jessie Willcox Smith. "Indoors," 1909.
14	Tony Johannot. "Story Telling," 1846.
15	Alan Wright. From *Two Little Kittens*, n.d.
16	Laura Muntz. "The Children's Hour," c.1897.
17	E. Stuart Hardy.
	From *Our New Story Book*, c.1910.
18	Henry Ryland.
	From *Hearts and Voices: Songs of the Better Land*, c.1898.
19	Joseph Henry Hatfield. "Mother Goose Stories," 1892.
20	Maginel Wright Barney. Magazine illustration, 1929.
21	Frederick Warren Freer. "Mother and Child Reading", n.d.
22	Cecile Walton. From *Nightlights*, 1929.
23	Unknown. From *A Friend For Little Children*, c.1890.
24	Ambrose Dudley. From *Nister's Holiday Annual*, c.1906.
25	James Francis Day. "Storytime," n.d.
26	W. Kay Blacklock. "The Story,"
	From *The After-You Story Book*, 1922.
27	Elsa Kaji. From *Rhymes of Golden Childhood*, 1922.

28   Gustave Doré. From *Les Contes de Perrault*, 1862.

29   Mary Cassatt. "Augusta Reading to her Daughter," 1910.

30   J.G. From *Good Times for the Little Ones*, 1887.

31   Francis Harrison.
     From *The Big Book of Pictures and Stories*, c.1920.

32   Florence and Margaret Hoopes.
     From *Through the Green Gate*, 1939.

33   Elise H. Stewart. From *Round the Clock*, c.1910.

34   Winifred Green. From *Mrs. Leicester's School*, c.1880.

35   Marguerite Davis. From *The Children's Own Readers*, 1929.

36   Lorentz Froelich.
     From *Les Premères Armes de Mademoiselle Lili*, c.1869.

37   Marguerite Davis. From *The Children's Own Readers*, 1929.

38   Unknown. From *Hello, David*, 1944.

39   Ruth M. Hallock and others.
     From *Fact and Story Readers*, 1930.

40   Winifred Bromhall.
     From *Stocking Tales: a Books of Stories for Children*, 1937.

41   Mary LaFetra Russell. From *Happy Hours*, 1917.

42   Edna Potter. From *In Storm and Sunshine*, 1938.

43   Jemima. "Hugh and William Reading in the Drawing Room
     at Roshven, (detail)" c.1860.

44   Florence and Margaret Hoopes.
     From *Childhood Readers: Stories for Every Day*, 1933.

45   Christian Krohg. "Østenfor Sol Og Vestenfor Måne," 1887.

46   Harry Wingfield. From *Talkabout Bedtime*, 1977.

47   Clara Olmstead. From *Two Little Kittens*, n.d.

Back Cover   Jessie Willcox Smith. Magazine illustration,